How I Lea1

How I Learned to Code

Lessons from teaching myself web development and becoming a paid programmer in only 3 months

A Short Memoir by Christopher R Dodd

How I Learned to Code

Table of Content

Preface	III
Chapter 1: Starting With My 'Why?'	1
Chapter 2: The 'How' Of Learning To Code	7
Chapter 3: Getting Hired	22
Chapter 4: The Struggles Of A Junior Developer	32
Chapter 5: Beginnings Of A Freelance Career	40
Chapter 6: Departure	51
Closing Remarks	56
Extra Resources	58
Questions & Answers	59

How I Learned to Code

Preface

First off, I want to thank you for picking up this copy of '*How I Learned to Code*'.

Learning to code was the best career decision I have ever made and even helps me today with my own personal projects and current role. I believe that regardless of what you choose to do with your programming skills, you'll be learning something that is fast becoming an essential skill.

In this book, I'll cover how I got started learning web development using free tools and how you can too. I'll also cover how I got my first developer job within 3 months and my tips for how you can get hired as quickly as possible (if that's what you want).

I will also mention before we begin that the title of the book is called '*How I learned to Code*' and not '*How to Code*' for a reason. If you're specifically looking for a guidebook on how to learn a particular language or framework, unfortunately this book may not be for you. Instead, this book is part memoir and part advice.

In fact, each chapter is broken up into both a story section and an advice section. I decided to write the book this way to help you get the most out of it. I believe that in each chapter, there are takeaways that may not be obvious to some readers and therefore, each passage of my journey will be accompanied by a piece of relevant advice.

Finally, as this book will be published on Amazon, I'd appreciate it if you could leave a positive review so that other people may find it easier. This is of course, only if you found the book valuable yourself. If not, please email me directly at chris@christhefreelancer.com. I strive to provide the very best content for my readers and if you find that the book is lacking anything at all, please let me know so I can include updates for future editions.

Ok, with all that out of the way, let's get straight into it!

How I Learned to Code

Chapter 1: Starting with my 'Why?'

Sitting at my fourth internship in Accounting, I had three big questions on my mind.

1. What will I do after university?
2. What my career will be in?, and
3. What do I want my life to look like?

To understand where my mind was at that exact moment, I'll need to give you some context.

At the time, I was a university student studying Accounting but with an insatiable need to travel the world after 6 months studying abroad in the US. I had been disillusioned by the fact that the students of my generation would have to deal with the reality of high unemployment and so I chose what seemed to be the most reliable career choice, a profession with approximately 98 percent graduate hiring rate.

In reality, I had spent the last 5 years of my life up to this point experimenting with different careers. I had been to 3 different universities, studied a variety of different degree paths and yet I hadn't gotten any closer to figuring out the answer to any of these three big questions.

I only knew two things:

How I Learned to Code

1. I wanted to travel, meet new people and experience the world, and
2. I wanted to finally be moving forward in my career

For the longest time, these goals seemed at opposite ends. On the travel side, I weighed up all the options like working on cruise ships, WOOFing or doing working holidays in Canada. On the career side, I knew that I didn't want a corporate career so it seemed that working in startups was the better path for me.

To be honest, my *'Learn to Code'* journey didn't really begin in March of 2015, but back when I was 12 years old, writing super basic HTML websites and setting them up on free hosts. I knew that after looking back on my childhood, there were indicators that a career as a web developer could be an appropriate path for me however, it wasn't until I began working on my accounting escape plan that I revisited programming. This was around late 2014.

I started with PHP and coded a very basic landing page that gathered emails addresses for a startup idea that I had. The idea at the time was not to become a professional web developer but to learn the skills to help me to build a startup. It wasn't until January 2015 that I stopped dabbling and started taking it seriously.

How I Learned to Code

Enter Pieter Levels

Around January 27 2016, I came across an article called *'This Guy is Starting 12 Startups in 12 Months'* on the website techinasia.com. I was initially drawn to the headline due to my interest in startups but as I read further, I found that the article resonated with me on so many more levels (no pun intended).

> "To Levels, it was a dream come true to be able to put both his work and love for travel together. His wanderlust originated from an exchange program back in 2009, when he was still a student:"
>
> - Daniel Tay, Tech in Asia

Like Levels, I had caught the travel bug after an exchange program abroad and like him, I wanted to launch my own startups. At this stage of my life, it was Levels who represented the perfect match of what I wanted to become.

Within days I became convinced. I decided with as much conviction as I have ever mustered that I would be become a web developer and travel the world with my girlfriend, Denise in 2016.

What's your Motivation?

If I could give someone only one piece of advice, it would be this:

Find your motivation

For me, becoming motivated enough was the biggest thing that has ever held me back from doing anything, especially learning to code. All the technicalities of how I got started, that I will discuss in this book, would have meant nothing without motivation.

For those of you who are considering a career in code, you need to be convinced that you will become a developer or at the very least, learn that you don't like it and move on as soon as possible.

As I will stress throughout this book, the job market for developers is crazy hot. I'm hoping I don't need to shower you with evidence, graphs and statistics to convince you of this. If you don't believe me, I'm sure you can find that information online.

Being a developer is one of those skills where you'll never be out of work as long as you are keeping up to date with your skills. I know this from my own experience, as well as from meeting

How I Learned to Code

numerous other developers over the course of my career.

How is that...
- An accounting student like me gets hired as a Junior Ruby on Rails developer after only a few short months of study
- My friend Guido is allowed to work only 3 days per week from a beach in Thailand for a major Dutch Bank, or
- A 34 year-old Internal Auditor (my friend, Dylan) can study coding on the side while working full-time, score a job and travel the world, working on his laptop, all in under 18 months

The reason: A booming job market.

I'll get into how I got hired in the coming chapters but for now, I wanted to stress the number one determinant of your success and that is, your drive.

Do you want to:
- Achieve financial security through a career with immense long-term potential?
- Work from anywhere in the world?
- Have flexible hours and work from home?
- Create amazing apps and websites that will change the world?

How I Learned to Code

Before moving onto Chapter 2, I want you to find what your motivation is. The only way you are going to fail in your pursuit of learning to code is to not give it a fair go. I'm asking you, not to dabble but to make the time to put the work in and always remember your own 'Why'?

Are you motivated? Are you ready? Let's go.

Chapter 2: The 'How' of Learning to Code

Websites to Help you Learn

Finding resources to learn how to code is not hard. Just do a quick Google search for the term, *'Learn to code'* and you'll see a list of websites and blog articles appear. From here you'll find numerous free resources such as:
- Code Academy - http://codeacademy.com
- Free Code Camp - https://www.freecodecamp.com/
- Envato Tuts - https://code.tutsplus.com/
- Plus many more

If you're happy to pay a little extra, you can get started using the following websites for an affordable monthly fee:
- Code School ($29 per month) - http://www.codeschool.com/
- Team Treehouse ($25 per month) - https://teamtreehouse.com/
- Lynda ($35 per month) - http://lynda.com, or
- Code Avengers ($29 per month) - https://www.codeavengers.com/

Finally, If you've got some big dollars to spend and are looking for the best of best, check out a paid mentorship program like Thinkful (https://www.thinkful.com/). If you want to buy an individual course, you can find a bunch of them on a course marketplace like Udemy (http://udemy.com) from $20 up to $200 each.

Other online education websites that include coding courses include:
- Khan Academy - https://www.khanacademy.org/
- Coursera - https://www.coursera.org, and
- edX - https://www.edx.org/

Not to mention, YouTube which is another great resource for learning code that's also completely free.

Other Resources

After posting my video on YouTube also entitled '*How I Learned to Code*', I received a range of questions on the subject of coding. In this section, I will address a few of the most common ones.

What about Books?

Books are another good resource for learning code but it depends on your learning style. For me personally, I prefer learning on the computer and having either a video or application walk me through it. From my perspective, it doesn't make sense to read something so practical off a page in a book if you're going to be doing it on a computer anyway. My friend Dylan on the other hand, had success with books and mentorships. It's simply different strokes for different folks.

What about Getting a Degree?

If you've been following me for some time, you would know that I don't recommend university to anyone unless your goal is to work for a major corporation like IBM or Google. Maybe that is what you want and that's cool but for the rest of us who just want to get started in our careers, getting a degree is the slowest and most expensive path to becoming a paid programmer.

University by nature is highly theoretical. It's structure is general and it's not self-paced. If you want to become a paid programmer, what you need is training. What you need is the practical skills; not just a broad understanding of the fundamentals of computer science (although that will of course help).

People always ask me: *"How long will I have to study code before I get hired"*? And the answer is simple, as long as it takes you to learn. It's completely self-paced. University has a set program length - a three-year degree, a 1 year diploma - but if you teach yourself through books and online platforms there's no limitation to how quickly you can learn the skills - It's completely up to you.

What Language / Framework should I learn?

This is another all-too-common question and unfortunately there is no one answer. Just look at the YouTube comments on either of the videos I mentioned previously. Everyone's got their own opinion. The important thing here is to ask yourself; What kind of software do you want to create? Do you want to make games, build websites or create the next Snapchat?

When we get into the story part of this chapter, I will tell you guys how I made my decision on what to learn but you don't have to follow me at all - in fact, you probably shouldn't. Telling you what language or framework to learn is much like telling someone what instrument to play. It's more important to ask what kind of music do you want to make.

In my video '*How to Become a Developer and Go Remote*', I recommended that the audience understand what their goals were in order to make a decision. For example, if you are just looking to get hired, you might want to look into learning a language/framework that has a lot of market demand.

How I Learned to Code

Note: I'll will explain the difference between languages and frameworks in the next section

The tech industry moves so fast these days but at the time of writing, the most popular languages and frameworks for web developers are:

How I Learned to Code

Languages	Frameworks
Javascript (essential for front-end but becoming increasingly used for back-end)	AngularJS, ReactJS, Ember JS, Backbone, Node.js, Meteor.js (the list is ever-growing)
Python	Django
PHP	Codeigniter, Symfony, Laravel, Yii 2, CakePHP
Ruby	Ruby on Rails, Sinatra

As most of my experience as a developer comes from building for the web, my research and expertise hasn't extended far into the world of desktop and phone apps. But if you're interested in making phone and desktop apps instead, check out...

- Swift for IOS development,
- Java for Android development,
- Swift or Objective-C for Mac OS X development, and
- C# for Windows development

Back-End vs Front-End

An important concept to understand in web development is the difference between back-end

How I Learned to Code

and front-end. This is where it gets a bit technical.

The front-end (otherwise known as the client-side) is everything you see in your browser. All the code on this layer is entirely public - if you don't believe me, right-click on a web page and click *'View Page Source'*. Everything you see on the front-end is a bunch of HTML, CSS and Javascript (as well as fonts and other assets) that have been sent to your browser by the back-end.

The back-end (also known as the server-side) is the private application layer that decides on what you'll see on the front-end. This is the layer that interacts with the database. If you login to a website, this is the layer that takes your details, finds a match in the database and returns to the front-end with the information that is unique to your account. Here, you can program in any language you like as this code never makes it to the browser.

As the web evolves, we're now seeing the distinction between the front-end and the back-end blurring. You might remember 5 to 10 years ago when you clicked on a link, it would always load a new page. Nowadays, websites are becoming more like applications where the front-end and the back-end are in constant interaction.

How I Learned to Code

Javascript is a perfect example of programming language which has historically sat on the front-end but is now used increasingly as a back-end language, further reducing the distinction between the front and back end.

Like I said, it's quite technical and you will learn the difference as you start to gain experience as a web developer. The important thing to decide starting out is whether you will focus on the back end, the front end or both (the full stack).

As you will hear in the following chapters, I quickly learnt after my first job that I definitely preferred the front-end as I like to see my work performing in the browser. You may be different. My advice, if you're not sure about which route to go down is to try both.

The Difference between a Language, a Framework and a Library

Another important concept to understand is the difference between a language, a framework and a library.

This is an answer from StackOverflow which I think sums it up perfectly.

How I Learned to Code

20 A language is syntax, grammar, semantics (and perhaps a core library) that implementers are required to support. A framework is a *cohesive set of library code that together simplifies* programming in any given language.

share improve this answer   edited Sep 21 '10 at 18:31   answered Sep 21 '10 at 17:56

mquander
42.5k ● 10 ● 77 ● 113

The difference is perhaps hard to explain but what I can say is that the language is what you start with.

Let's say you want to program on the back-end and you decide PHP is a good choice. While you can create an application without a framework using PHP, you usually wouldn't want to. This is because there are certain things that are common with each application (things like authentication and authorisation for example). This is where it helps to build code on top of a framework. It forces you to adhere to a structure and saves you time on creating functionality that is common with almost every app.

Libraries on the other hand, are modular sets of code that you can add when you want to create a functionality without spending a lot of time coding from scratch. They can also help to simplify how you write code. An example from jQuery (a popular Javascript library) demonstrates this well...

// find all paragraphs with the class "summary" in the article with ID "first"
Using Regular JS:
var n = document.querySelectorAll("article#first p.summary");
Using jQuery:
var n = $("article#first p.summary");

Note: If you decide to learn how to code JS on the front-end, you should become familiar with jQuery very quickly.

Again, as you gain experience, you will begin to better understand the distinction between these core concepts. So, don't be worried, these are all things that you will learn.

Like I said in the preface, this is not a theoretical guide book to learning code but I wanted to just give a quick overview of a few important concepts. If that was all a bit too technical, don't worry! From now on, we're back to the story.

How did I Learn to code?

Most of the websites I listed at the start of this chapter I have tried out at different times however, there was one website the formed the foundation of each language/framework I ever

How I Learned to Code

learned. That website of course, is Lynda.com, a multi-billion dollar training library with courses on everything from graphic design to business principles, not just programming.

I found that Lynda provided a really strong foundation as the instructors talked not just about how to do things but why. Even in something as practical as coding, you still need to know the reason behind what you're doing. That's why you should never learn from someone who just gives you step-by-step instructions without guiding you through the actual thought process.

Apart from doing a few basic courses on front-end development with Code Academy, my first proper programming course I ever did was *"PHP with MySQL Essential Training"* (which you can find here: http://bit.ly/2bkZTyP). After that course, I was able to code that landing page project I mentioned in Chapter 1.

Unfortunately, the website I created is no longer online but what I can say is that it was quite basic. It was comprised of just three pages, the first: a the landing page where I had my 'Call-to-action", a few selling points and a box to leave your email, the second: a page that thanked the user for submitting their email and invited them to invite their friends via email and finally, the "Thank you" page. I coded the whole thing basically from scratch and the biggest thing I learned from the whole process was just how unnecessary that was.

Let me explain...

Side note: Programming is modular

An important thing to understand when developing any application or website is that programming is modular. Programming languages are wonderful. They allow us to write code in a more "human" way but at the core of any piece of software is just ones and zeros. Everything you will create as a developer will be created on top of an ever evolving infrastructure.

Why are you telling me this Chris?

I make the point that programming is modular because I want you to understand that you don't have to build everything from scratch. In fact, you shouldn't.

When I did my first project, I used a PHP library to take a visitor's email, insert it into a database and then send them out an email. It was a good learning experience but the truth is that I didn't need to do this. Instead, I could have used any of the numerous email automation services to do this all for me - for free (example: MailChimp (http://mailchimp.com)).

This is why we use frameworks, as things like authentication and authorisation (having a login system), database connections and page layouts are very common but laborious to set up without a framework or library.

Anyways, back to the story!

Choosing What to Learn

In 2014 when I coded that landing page, I just used PHP because it was the most familiar to me. Nowadays, many people will tell you that PHP is on the way out. I can't confirm or deny that but in 2015 when I decided to pursue web development as a career, I was after one thing - a job.

I tossed and turned for a while, trying to figure out what would be the best language/framework to learn and had almost decided on learning Javascript with Node.js until I discovered a meetup at my local coworking space called *"Ruby on Rails: Installfest"*.

The installfest was simply an event where Ruby on Rails (RoR) experts met up with newbies to help them get set up with RoR and get started on their first application. It was here that I was exposed to RoR community in my home city of Brisbane, I got to ask a bunch of questions and ended up deciding to pursue RoR as my language/framework of choice.

The Power of The Developer Community

If you want to get hired, push through barriers and get the most out of your 'Learn to code' journey then you should definitely make an effort to connect with the appropriate developer community.

From my experience, the culture amongst developers is amazingly collaborative. Through meetups and online chat, I have met strangers that will happily take an hour out of their day to help me with whatever coding challenge I may have, connect me with opportunities or just chat about new languages or technology with me. Just look at the incredible amount of free software out there, much of which is completely open-source.

Tapping into the developer community is a massive advantage yet quite easy to do. Just search for meetups in your local area about different programming languages using Meetup.com, seek out developer forums or join chat groups on apps like Slack (http://slack.com).

Through the RoR installfest event, I discovered a strong community around the Ruby language in my home city of Brisbane. Each month, RoR developers would meet at a suburban library to listen to guest speakers talk about programming and then network over dinner straight after. It was here that I found my first job.

How I Learned to Code

Chapter 3: Getting Hired

After the RoR installfest, I got to work learning Ruby using Lynda.com and attended my first BrisRuby meetup (the monthly meeting for Ruby developers in Brisbane) about a week later.

Side note: full list of courses I took are on the website at http://christhefreelancer.com/recommended-resources

I'll never forget the first meetup because it's where I met my first boss, Nigel. He was the chief organiser of the meetup and a co-founder of a local RoR programming firm.

The meetup began with Nigel making a few community announcements before heading into the talks for the evening. Just before the speaker came on stage, Nigel asked the group (about 10-20 people) if any companies were hiring or if anyone in the crowd was looking for work. I put my hand up.

I was honest with the group. I had just started learning Ruby about a week previous and I was almost certainly too much of a beginner to get hired but I told them that my goal was to get hired down the track. After the talks had finished and the post-meetup dinner had concluded,

How I Learned to Code

Nigel handed me his card and asked me to send him an email for a possible job.

I had just been given an amazing opportunity. I obviously had zero experience and only a few weeks of RoR study under my belt yet I must have demonstrated my drive and ambition quite well. I made sure that I wouldn't let this opportunity slide and I became even more motivated to study Ruby and get hired with Nigel's company.

The next stage was not a traditional interview but a series of short chats with the company's other founder, Sean and a coding challenge that I spent two days on. The following is the actual brief that Nigel sent me:

How I Learned to Code

Hi Chris,

For our tech review process, can you please create the following Rails app for discussion during our meeting.

"Build a Rails app which has companies and each company can have multiple contacts. Add the ability for a contact to be related to any other contact in that company."

I look forward to seeing you on Monday.

Cheers,

Nigel

May 7 2015

On Monday, the 11th of May 2015, roughly one week after I was given the challenge, I met with the two founders at the office in East Brisbane to evaluate my work.

How I Learned to Code

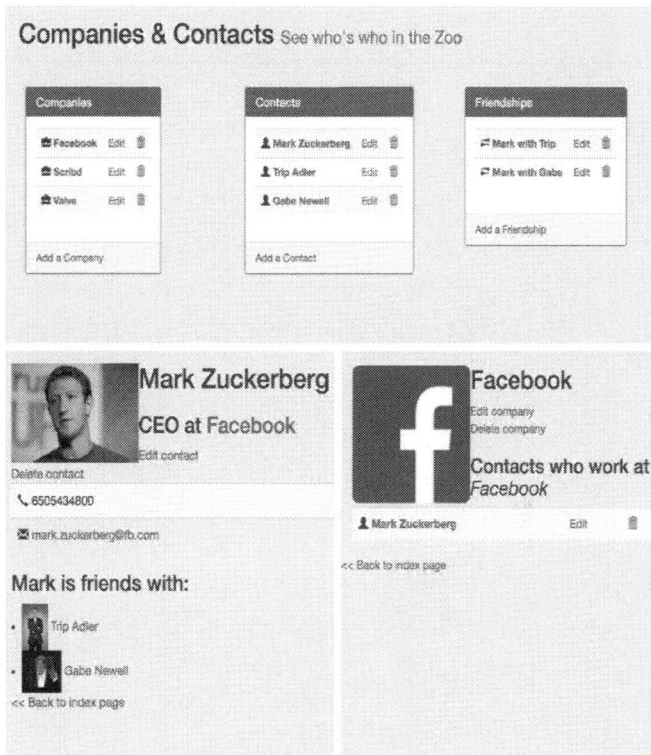

I had spent almost half my time on the front-end, making the app responsive (as in, working well on any size screen) and using nice icons but Nigel hadn't seen any of it. He literally only looked at the code! The other founder, Sean was the one who asked Nigel to actually show the app in the browser so that he could navigate it. The collage above features some of the pages on the app.

How I Learned to Code

There were a few critiques included in the evaluation but overall, I wasn't sure how I had done. The only thing I knew was that I had spent perhaps way too long making the front-end look presentable.

After the first meeting, I was invited back to office for another one on Friday. I grew excited. This had to be it! What else could it be? I had met with the team, done a coding challenge and talked to the founders. This Friday's meeting could only mean one thing, it had to be an offer!

That Friday, I sat in Sean's office where I got what I wanted, an official offer for a full-time position as a Junior Ruby Developer with a salary of $50,000 AUD inclusive of superannuation (compulsory retirement fund) starting June 1st 2015.

After a long process of meetings and code tests, I was so relieved. I had finally gotten a job as a developer within 3 months of taking my first RoR course on Lynda! I had surprised everyone especially my dad who said I was crazy to think that I could get a job without any formal training. But, as you'll hear in the next chapter, there was a big downside to getting hired so soon and in reality, the real challenge was only just about to begin.

How I Learned to Code

Advice for those seeking their first job as a developer

First of all, I don't want you to think that 3 months is an average time period to get your first job after you start learning. Of course, there's no barrier to how quickly you can get hired apart from your own ability to learn and the time you dedicate to it but I would use 12 months as a more realistic timeline.

Your ability to get hired will come down to a few important factors:

1. The Job Market in Your Area

Keep in mind that as an Australian, I'm writing from a westerner's perspective, living in a modern city of about 2 million people. I can't guarantee that there are jobs available in your local area but what I can say with confidence is that, as a generalisation, the world needs more developers.

To use my own story as an example, I'm sure some of you may be wondering how I got hired so quickly. The truth is that Nigel and Sean's previous hire lasted only a few months before he was hired by an even bigger company. Rather than look for another talented developer, they looked for someone who was driven and would relish the opportunity.

Like I said in the first chapter, talented developers will never be out of a job and employers will offer unrivalled benefits to attract and retain skilled developers. Companies like Sean and Nigel's were perhaps too small to attract and retain highly motivated and highly skilled workers so they had to invest in someone like me.

2. Your Enthusiasm and Motivation

Apart for the wildy hot job market for developers in Australia, I attribute the majority of my success to demonstrating my drive and commitment. It was one of the first times in my life that I became highly motivated to achieve a professional goal and I made my intentions clear from the start that I wanted to become a developer.

3. Putting Yourself Out There

All the opportunity in the world amounts to nothing if you are not putting yourself out there. How could my first employers have known that I was a good fit if they hadn't met me first? I had no resume as a developer and my degree was completely unrelated.

What instantly set me apart was that I was the only beginner programmer that regularly attended the BrisRuby meetup. How could you miss me in a group of only 20 people? It still baffles me today how there were no other university students looking for a job at this meetup. I virtually had no competition!

So, take my story as a lesson and find where your local programming community hangs out. Programmers love to talk code and they're usually very willing to help you out. The developer community is an incredibly powerful resource. Don't be shy, get out there!

4. Skills

Last on the list but of course also very important, is your skill level. Most employers won't care that you got an A on your last assignment. They can easily judge your skill by looking at your work. If you receive a code challenge like me, obviously do your absolute best but don't be too scared about making a mistake. If they've given you the opportunity, chances are that they want you to succeed, they just need to see that you have got some skills that they can work with.

The reason why skills is number 4 on the list is that you'll never quite master programming. Technology is constantly evolving and so must your skill level. The most important attribute that you need to have as a programmer is to be a problem-solver. There's a real chance that the

How I Learned to Code

specific way you write code today may be different next year but the ability to think like a programmer will remain. That's why the skills you build learning any type of programming will be highly transferable into others.

As a junior developer, employers won't expect you to know everything but they will expect that you have the potential to figure things out as you go.

All of this might come as a surprise to you if you're in the usual scarcity mindset of looking for a job. If that's the case, I can very much relate.

Before I tried to become a developer, I was one of the thousands of accounting students fighting over only a few hundreds 'good jobs'. I was like a lot of students my age, studying hard with no guarantees and with a lot to prove just to get my foot in the door.

Yes, we live in a time of automation, outsourcing and incredible technological disruption. Many professions are hiring less and less as computers and offshore workers take much of the work. There's a clear divide. You can either be on the side of technological disruption or working against it, it's really up to you.

Rather than feeling daunted by the mountain of never-ending skills that you will constantly strive

How I Learned to Code

to learn as a developer, embrace the fact that employers are waiting for you to be just good enough to hire you. They want you to succeed, all you have to do is be good enough to do the job at hand. So remember, learn as much as you can, go where the jobs are and put yourself out there. If you do all of that, I can't see why you can't get hired.

Chapter 4: The Struggles of a Junior Developer

Like any job, the moment you get hired is when the work truly begins but as a junior developer with less than 3 months of self-directed study under my belt, I was really thrown into the deep-end.

The good thing about self-paced learning is that you can continually push yourself above your skill level, ever so slightly and comfortably build your skillset. If a solution you find online is too challenging, you might back away and try something else. When on the job however, you're working with other people, existing code and libraries that you may not be familiar with.

The Culture of Developers

After my first week at my new job, I wrote the following in my personal journal:

> "The guys I work with are thoroughbred coders. They'd been doing it a long time and they were fully emerged in the culture. They almost perfectly fit the stereotype of computer geeks, I don't. To me coding is just a skill. I'm growing to accept that I don't appreciate the scene as

> much as my fellow developers but for now, I am one of them." - May 6th 2015

I was only 5 days into my new career and already, I was starting to feel overwhelmed.

I obviously had a bunch of questions. Virtually everything was new to me. I thought I knew a fair bit but I was quickly realising just how big of a 'noob' I really was.

The other thing I was noticing was that my coworkers were really pumped about code. They lived and breathed it. While I was needing a break after 8 hours of staring at a screenful of code, they were at home working on other projects or reading books to learn more.

Despite being busy on their own tasks, when they took the time to help me through an issue, they explained important concepts to me in such detail and with so much passion. I admired them for it but felt increasingly out of place given that I was nowhere near as passionate as they were.

> "The first few weeks at my job have been tough. While I wondered for the first few weeks whether I'd made the right choice, I've now realised that I'm only irritated when I'm bored or struggling to solve problems. As I grow more competent, I'm

> feeling better and now the goal is to continue to get better." - June 17th 2015

To be honest, I really struggled. This job was the first time ever that I had been employed full-time and I wasn't sure how to view it.

> "Just a few weeks into my first full time job and already, I feel like I need a career change. I'm unlike everyone else at work in almost every way. I can't get excited about object decorators and the like. In that sense, I don't think I am a true programmer." - June 28th 2015

As the days went on, I continued to write passages in my journal like the one above, assuring myself that the feelings would pass. I really didn't want to give up, especially after placing so much importance on getting the job in the first place.

On the 8th of July 2015 however, I started to seriously consider quitting. I even talked it over with my boss Sean but he reassured me that they would continue to patient with me.

> "As the day goes on, the pressure begins to mount again. Nigel is frustrated with my lack of understanding and I'm growing anxious. I don't want to do this anymore. If the expectation is going to

continue to rise, I am not going to last. Even though Sean says that it's 'all good', the vibe outside in the dev room is much different. I decided that come tomorrow, I will talk to Sean to resign." - July 9th 2015

The day I resigned was an awkward and sad goodbye. Although I was obliged to give 2 weeks notice, Sean saw little point in having me stick around and so I wrapped up my small project that I was working on and left for good before lunchtime.

Now, before you close this book and throw it across the room, keep reading as there's a silver lining to this story. As we'll get into in the next chapter, leaving that job turned out to be the right thing to do and what happened a few months later turned out to be the real dream come true. So please keep reading!

My Advice for Newbies

As much as I like to sit here and tell you about how awesome it is to be a developer, the truth is that coding may simply not be for you. There's also the possibility that certain types of programming or languages work well with how you think while others may not.

How I Learned to Code

There are Many Types of Programming

In my video with Dylan Wolff entitled '*How to Become a Developer and Go Remote*' (freely available on YouTube), Dylan touched on an important point that I hadn't thought too much about.

> "I think you need to find something that interests you. I started learning a bit of Javascript initially and the syntax just confused me and it wasn't code that I enjoyed writing. I discovered Ruby and that was something I did enjoy. So, I imagine there's work out there for any programming language you want to learn but it needs to be something you enjoy writing." - Dylan Wolff, 'How to Become a Developer and Go Remote', July 23 2016

Up until this point in my story, I had been narrow-minded. All I wanted was to be a developer but there are simply so many types. I judged my decision on what to learn completely on the level of demand and not on what I enjoyed learning.

If you find that don't like your first experience as a programmer, try another language! Rather than think programming isn't for you, try to come at it from a different angle.

How I Learned to Code

While Dylan and I were both developers, we were each very different in what we enjoyed. He loves working on the back-end and I prefer the front-end. Neither is the better way to do it and you should do your best to discover what works for you personally.

As you'll hear in the next chapter, I ended up finding a different language/framework to Ruby on Rails that I enjoyed working with much more. For yourself, it's possible you might feel that coding is not for you and I understand. I had these same thoughts throughout my coding journey.

To be honest, my motivation to code came predominantly from my desire to work remotely, however, there are many ways to achieve the digital nomad lifestyle without coding.

Make sure to think about your own motivations when deciding what to get into. While there are amazing benefits to being a developer, I think it would be incredibly naïve to say that everyone should be one.

My intention here of course, is not to turn you away from learning code - I believe that we all need to know at least some. Instead, I think it's important to know when to try something else. Just make sure to try a few different things (ie.

languages, frameworks, etc) before you completely write it off.

Know Yourself

The other key learning from my first job was that I simply didn't fit in.

The culture of the Sean & Nigel's firm was complete Ruby obsession. My interest was different, I wanted to create apps and see my work performing beautifully in the browser, not just passing 3,000 code tests. The focus at the firm however, was completely back-end and my coworkers would stay up late to solve a coding challenge just because they were *that* into it.

I remember Nigel telling me that he would sit in his bed late at night, furiously trying to solve a coding challenge, unable to sleep until he figured it out. I did not share that obsession and that's why I grew increasingly concerned that I was out of place.

Most people go through life trying to make themselves fit into a certain group rather than find a group in which they already match well with. In my first job, I was trying to fit a square peg in a circular hole and it just wasn't working. It's important that you consider that this could also be the case for you but more importantly, understand that it doesn't mean that you're not

How I Learned to Code

meant to be a developer if your first job just doesn't work out.

In the next chapter, I'll tell you how I continued my coding journey, started freelancing and found my ideal web development job in just a few more months.

Chapter 5: Beginnings of a Freelance Career

By the time I had left my first job as a programmer, I had finished my degree in Accounting but it was too late to apply for graduate positions. Even still, I had already decided that I wasn't going to pursue a career in accounting anymore. I still wanted to be a digital nomad and therefore, I had to find something I could do remotely.

Despite spending a good part of the year focused specifically on coding, I began to look for something else. My first job had made me feel like I wasn't up to the challenge of being a full-time developer and once again, I was back to square one.

It wasn't until I started to look into creating my own blog a few months later that I ended up coming full-circle and returning to web development as I realised that I did still enjoy coding and making websites. It was here that I had the realisation that it wasn't necessarily coding that was the wrong path for me but the particular type of programming that I decided to pursue.

The process of designing and developing my own blog was so enjoyable that I decided to start freelancing as a wordpress developer. Wordpress was the framework that I had built all of my blogs on in the past (and still do) and happens to be the most popular CMS for clients who need a rather basic website.

The Power of Coworking

Many people ask me questions about freelancing. The most common perhaps, is how to actually find work. I admit it. It's tough! If you want to build a long-term freelance career these days, I believe you need two things:

1. A reputation for delivering quality work, and
2. An attraction model (usually your own personal brand) that connects you with possible clients

In my experience, working with small clients on a variety of jobs is a very hard business to sustain. Most of my success has come through longer term contracts but one thing that every single freelance gig or contract I have ever gotten has in common is that it has all come through a connection to a coworking space (apart from a small amount of work through UpWork).

Coworking, I guess you could say is my *'secret sauce'*. Without coworking, I probably wouldn't

How I Learned to Code

be here today, writing this sentence in a cafe in Saigon after 8 months of work and travel.

Remember when I said that I attended my first RoR Installfest at my local coworking space? Well, that space is called River City Labs (RCL) and after my first job had ended, I was back to working out of there whenever I could.

I met my first client Ricardo through a small study group called startup school that met each Tuesday morning. I helped him implement authentication on his Wordpress website for a small fee of $150 AUD.

After Ricardo, I helped a creative agency next door to RCL with some spillover, creating a basic website to display on a tablet at a tennis conference. That job was worth about $500 AUD.

Clients were few and far between and it didn't take me long to realise that I was going to go broke if I didn't get something more regular really soon.

I spoke to a recruiter friend of mine who I'd met through Startup Weekend at RCL to see if she could help me out. Coincidentally, something had just come across her desk. It was a 5 week, full-time contract with TAFE (ie. Technical and Further Education) converting word documents into HTML pages. It all sounded great apart from one small detail. The office was on the Sunshine Coast, an approximate 1.5 hour drive from where I lived in Brisbane! I had no other option, I sucked it up and signed the contract.

Working at TAFE - My first full-time contract

Working at TAFE was the complete opposite of my first web development job. It was so little of a challenge that it was just mindless. I remember telling the clients at the end of the contract that it was so easy that virtually anyone with basic computer skills could learn to do the job within one week.

I can't say I enjoyed the whole experience too much. Apart from the crazy commute (3+ hours a day), the work was so boring that I'd daydream constantly about breaking out of the cubicle. I would sit there depressed about having to be in this position. I even questioned my decision to leave the first job I had. But, in terms of a lifespan, 5 weeks was a small amount of time and after the work at TAFE was done, I was back in Brisbane with some more savings but still a lot of work to do.

How I Learned to Code

Returning to River City Labs

I happily returned to River City Labs and got back to work, looking for more clients and contracts. While TAFE was something I could put on my resume, I learned no new skills from the whole experience and so, I was back to where I started (yet again).

Luckily, a change was coming and I was about to catch a big break.

A fresh gig had just come in, creating a Dog Park listing website similar to doggo.com.au for a startup that connects pet owners with pet sitters and vice versa. The founder Deborah wanted a dog park listing incorporated on the company's blog website as an extra feature for members.

I had no idea about what to charge but I estimated it would take me about two weeks with a full-time availability and so I made a conservative quote of $1,500 AUD.

In hindsight, I think I undercharged but as you'll soon read, the opportunity to work with Deborah's company would extend much further than this one gig.

The Comeback

As I began to wrap-up this job for Deborah's company, it was about September 2015, only a few months before our planned departure from Australia. I was now only just breaking even with my freelance work and the way I saw it, I had only 3 options:

1. I could look for a job as a casual waiter/bartender (my former 'career') and stack on as many hours as possible,
2. I could attempt to get a full-time job and quit after a few months (I didn't feel comfortable with this idea),
3. I could find a remote job (difficult with my current level of experience), or
4. I could find a 3 month full-time contract (probably the most ideal option)

I decided to head over Seek.com.au (the largest job search website in Australia) and look for all 4 of these options - It wasn't looking good. I had been neglecting my 'career' as a waiter to move onto bigger things and a remote job as a developer seemed a bit too far out of reach. When I searched for a 3 month contract however, guess who showed up? That's right! It was Deborah's company!

How I Learned to Code

It was the perfect job, full-time, 3 months duration and for an hourly rate of $50 AUD. My heart skipped a beat.

Usually I would have highly doubted that I could get a job like this but because I was already working for them as a freelancer, I felt I had amazing opportunity here.

Here's the email I sent to Chris, the CTO at the company:

How I Learned to Code

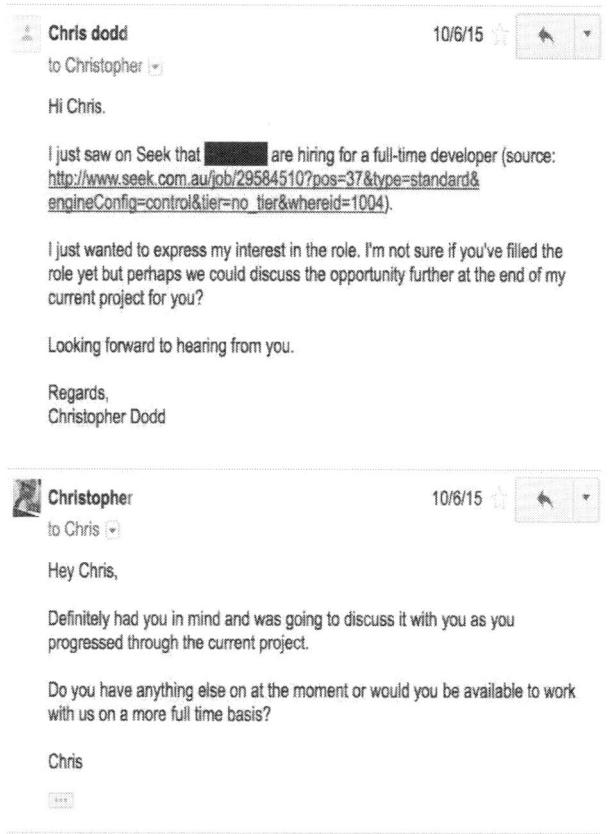

On Friday October 9th 2015, I visited the office to meet with Deborah and CTO Christopher. With the freelance project just wrapping up, the timing was perfect. We got to know each other and talked about the project.

Like any good job interview, it didn't feel like an interrogation. I looked a good fit for the role and they'd seen my work. The only thing that worried me was the big question, '*Was I ready?*'.

It wasn't long before I got a call back from Chris, "*Hey Chris, we'd like for you to work with us but we were wondering, due to your lack of experience whether you would accept $40 an hour instead?*" (I'm paraphrasing of course). I instantly accepted.

Amazingly, I had gone from working for Sean and Nigel for roughly $25, to TAFE for $30 and now Deborah's Startup for $40 AUD per hour! What's more, I had incredible flexibility, the ability to come to work any time in the morning and leave any time between 4 and 6pm. It was up to me. I got paid by the hour so as long as we were making progress, I could do a half-day or take a day off when I needed.

Besides a short period at the beginning of the contract where I started to relive some of the struggles from my first job, the contract went very smoothly. I was finally being challenged enough that I could still handle it whilst growing my skills along the way. And, I was now a part of a team which shared my motivation for code for the sake of creation not just code for the sake of code. There was only one thing remaining that was left unknown and that was how they would feel about keeping me on past the contract and allowing me to work as a remote developer.

How I Learned to Code
Luck & Opportunity

So, what did you learn from reading chapter 5?

I think some people have the inclination to tune out after they hear a story of luck and opportunity like mine. Maybe they say, *"Oh, he was just lucky. I can't do that!"* but there are some lessons here.

Yes, I've been very lucky at times but luck is just opportunity, it's what you do with the opportunity that will determine your success.

We're all lucky in some way. Going back further than my web development career, I was lucky just for having been born in Australia. I was lucky for being born healthy. I was lucky for being born in the digital era where all of this is only just become possible. Look around you, there is opportunity all around.

Once you identify where the opportunity lies, it's all about what you choose to do with it.

I knew that there were a lot of jobs for developers available in Australia but I wasn't going to find them by being stuck on my computer. I signed up at River City Labs, joined groups, attended startup weekends and worked on my own projects. I put myself out there and you can do the same.

How I Learned to Code

I'm sure you've heard the term, '*Create your own luck*' right? Well, to me, it means maximising your own opportunities. By working on my coding skills, I was creating opportunity for myself and by doing it at River City Labs, in the presence of others, I was creating more opportunities to get hired.

You may be reading this from an oppressed country, you may have little money or maybe you have some kind of learning disability. Don't let this deter you! Find where the opportunity lies and maximise it. The worst thing you can do after reading this book is to just give up. If you have a serious challenge however, that you feel is holding you back, feel free to send me an email at chris@christhefreelancer.com. I want to know what it is and how I can help.

Chapter 6: Departure

Things were going great at work and there was talk on the cards about my role extending past the short-term contract into a full-time position. If that was to be the case, I would have definitely accepted the offer as long as I could do it remotely.

The money I was saving was starting to grow to a good level but I knew I needed some kind of remote income to sustain my upcoming digital nomad journey. Nothing would be better than to continue working for Deborah's company.

Towards the end of my contract, I expected Deborah or the Co-Director of the company, Mark to ask me into the office to have a 'proper' discussion about it but it ended up happening in the lunch line at the cafeteria next door.

"So, what are your plans for after the contract?", asked Mark.

Without giving away too much, this was where I told him about our digital nomad plan. By the end of the conversation however, I still had no indication of how he or the rest of the team felt about it so I decided to wait. Surely they'd bring it up sooner or later.

How I Learned to Code

Bringing it up with Deborah

After hearing nothing, I decided that I was going to have to be the one to bring it up. I asked Deb for a chat and I told her that I would love to stay on if the opportunity presented itself but I already had a flight out of Brisbane and so I would need to be able to do it remotely.

The answer I got was rather vague. As the company was a startup, money was a constant worry and Deborah couldn't make any promises. She said that they'd love to keep me on if they could continue to afford it and this is where it got confusing.

From Deborah's perspective, my contract was ending and I would be finishing up just before I left for Bali. From my perspective, I thought it was safe to assume that I would continue working until I was told otherwise. There was still work to be done and I was already working past my contract end date.

Neither one of us were in the wrong but it did end up in a period of confusion when I left the office for the final time. The vibe from Deb was that this was goodbye but the idea I got from my development team was that I would still be working from next Monday. I sent her an email to clarify.

How I Learned to Code

To cut a long story short, I ended up working two and a half more weeks for Deborah's company, the first two weeks at the coworking space Hubud and the other few days at different coworking spaces featured in my third vlog.

When it all had ended, I made a post on my Facebook page:

How I Learned to Code

In terms of my '*Learn to code*' story, this was the post that celebrated the end of a long journey towards getting started as a digital nomad.

Advice for Going Remote

Perhaps one of the failings of my whole approach was that I wasn't clear with anyone that my intention was to go remote. I was just getting started and I felt like the remote thing was possibly too much to ask.

Without a job, I wouldn't have had the money to go travelling anyway. At the very least, I was concurrently building both skills and savings. Therefore, I can't say I regret any part of my approach.

If going remote is what you want to do, I need to be honest with you. From my experience, it's much easier to sort out how you are going to make money before you leave rather than doing it while you are already on the journey. I think it would be unwise to assume that you can find a job on the road that will offer you the kind of money and hours that I had working in Australia unless you're a very experienced developer.

My advice for newbie digital nomads is to be prepared but not over-prepared. You can rely on your savings to start with but I would recommend getting some momentum going in terms of accumulating location independent income before you leave.

A great example of this is my friend, Dylan Wolff, who I mentioned earlier. He has a similar story to me but instead of waiting until the 11th hour to announce that he wanted to work remotely, he instead made it clear to employers and got a position at a firm that was very open to the idea of remote work.

If on the other hand, you plan to freelance, I'd make sure to have at least some ongoing client work before you leave.

Unfortunately for us newbies (I still consider myself a newbie), growing your career is hard enough whilst simultaneously trying to make it work on the road. You can approach it however you like but don't expect it to be easy. As I write this passage, I'm currently working harder than I ever have before but the difference is that I have a dream in mind and I wouldn't have it any other way.

Closing Remarks

It seems that many digital nomads stumble upon location independence almost accidentally. For me, it was a very conscious decision and it came at a time when I was just finishing university, had never been employed full-time and did not have a ton of money saved up.

I surprised a lot of people by making to the move out of Australia to live and work in South East Asia but the experience so far has been amazing. That's why I'm so passionate about helping others achieve the same lifestyle.

Now, your motivation might be different to mine. You may not be motivated by travel and that's fine. The process I went through to get started as a developer is not unique to someone with the sole intention of becoming location independent. I hope that regardless of your core motivation that you learned something valuable from my story.

For the few of you who are interested in what I'm doing now, I can tell you that it's no longer web development. About 4 months after leaving Australia, I met a location independent entrepreneur in Chiang Mai called Maxence who I now work for full-time as a digital marketer - but that of course, is another story.

How I Learned to Code

Despite no longer working as a developer, I still wouldn't have changed anything about my journey as it truly is what has gotten me here today. To me, developing is one of the only careers that is moving so fast that you can jump on the bandwagon right now and start building a career quicker than your colleagues at university trying to squeeze their way into a dying industry.

I said it before and I'll say it again, regardless of your motivation for learning to code, I don't think you'll regret trying it.

Best of luck, and be sure to keep in touch on social media!

Also, if you enjoyed the book, please leave a review on Amazon as this will help others to find it.

Until next time,
Christopher R Dodd

Facebook:
https://www.facebook.com/christhefreelancer
Twitter: https://twitter.com/ChrisRDodd
Instagram:
https://www.instagram.com/christhefreelancer
Snapchat: http://snapchat.com/add/christhefree

Extra Resources

My 4 Steps to Location Independence (Free eBook): http://bit.ly/2cUHWlA

The YouTube video that inspired the book by the same name: http://bit.ly/2d1IoRj

Dylan Wolff's Story
On the Blog: http://bit.ly/2cHiBoO
On the Podcast: http://bit.ly/2ctM2E1

My YouTube video on 'How to Become a Developer and Go Remote' (Q&A with Dylan Wolff)
http://bit.ly/2cZm50d

How I Learned to Code

Questions & Answers

Q: How much time per week did you spend learning before you got hired?

A: I was a student at the time with a part-time job but I had a few days off each week. I remember dedicating the whole of Tuesdays to learning and half of Thursday as these were the most reliable times I had off uni and work.

This question is one of the most common questions I get. If you have any extra questions about being a web developer in general, please watch my Q&A video (linked above). If you still have a question, send me an email at chris@christhefreelancer.com and I will do my best to answer. This section will likely expand as I receive more questions.

Printed in Great Britain
by Amazon